Dear Parent:
Your child's love of reading starts here!

Every child learns to read in a different way and at his or her own speed. Some go back and forth between reading levels and read favorite books again and again. Others read through each level in order. You can help your young reader improve and become more confident by encouraging his or her own interests and abilities. From books your child reads with you to the first books he or she reads alone, there are I Can Read Books for every stage of reading:

SHARED READING
Basic language, word repetition, and whimsical illustrations, ideal for sharing with your emergent reader

BEGINNING READING
Short sentences, familiar words, and simple concepts for children eager to read on their own

READING WITH HELP
Engaging stories, longer sentences, and language play for developing readers

READING ALONE
Complex plots, challenging vocabulary, and high-interest topics for the independent reader

ADVANCED READING
Short paragraphs, chapters, and exciting themes for the perfect bridge to chapter books

I Can Read Books have introduced children to the joy of reading since 1957. Featuring award-winning authors and illustrators and a fabulous cast of beloved characters, I Can Read Books set the standard for beginning readers.

A lifetime of discovery begins with the magical words "I Can Read!"

Visit www.icanread.com for information
on enriching your child's reading experience.

For D.B.H.,

the one and only

I Can Read Book® is a trademark of HarperCollins Publishers.

Mrs. Brice's Mice
Copyright © 1988 by Syd Hoff

Library of Congress Cataloging-in-Publication Data
Hoff, Syd, date
  Mrs. Brice's mice.
  (An I can read book)
  Summary: Mrs. Brice has twenty-five mice and they all do everything together.
  [1. Mice—Fiction.] I. Title. II. Series.
  ISBN 978-0-06-022452-3 (lib. bdg.) — ISBN 978-0-06-444145-2 (pbk.)
PZ7.H672Mhi 1988   87-45680
[E]—dc21   CIP
                                                AC

21 LSCC 55 54 53 52
❖

I Can Read! BEGINNING READING 1

MRS. BRICE'S MICE

Story and Pictures by

Syd Hoff

HARPER

An Imprint of HarperCollinsPublishers

Mrs. Brice had twenty-five mice.

She fed her mice
the finest cheese.

She washed and dried them

behind their ears,

so they were always clean.

Mrs. Brice loved to sing for them.
When she played the piano,
twenty-four little mice
danced around her.

One very small mouse
danced on top of her hand.
He was afraid to fall
between the keys.

9

When Mrs. Brice went to bed,

twelve little mice

slept on one side of her.

Twelve little mice

slept on the other side.

One very small mouse

slept on the clock,

in case he wanted to know

what time it was.

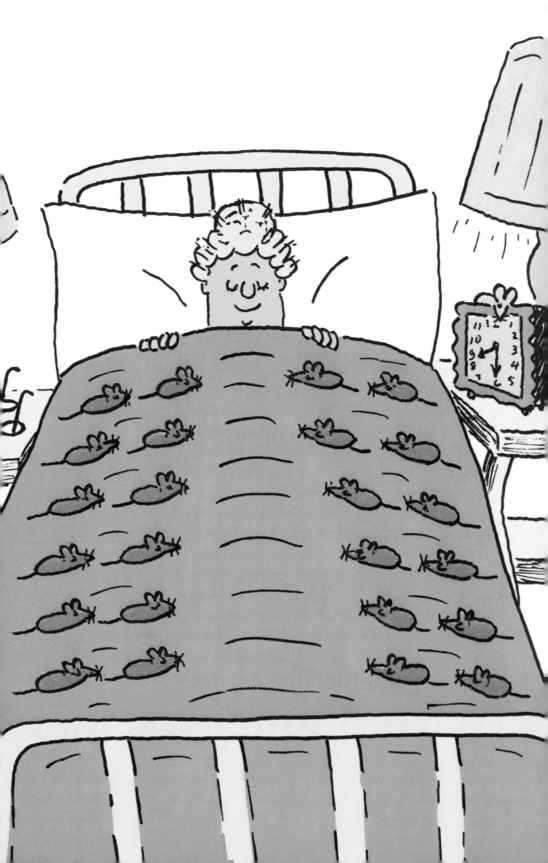

In the morning,

Mrs. Brice did exercises.

She stretched

her arms and legs.

She bent over

and touched her toes

with her fingers.

"One, two, three,
four, five, six . . .
One, two, three,
four, five, six . . ."

Twenty-four little mice

did exercises, too.

They stretched,

they bent,

they touched their toes.

One very small mouse

kept on sleeping.

"It is time for our walk,"
said Mrs. Brice.
Twelve little mice
walked in front of her.
Twelve little mice
walked in back.
One very small mouse
sat on top
of Mrs. Brice's hat,
so he could see
where they were going.

He saw a cat.

Twelve little mice
ran this way.
Twelve little mice
ran that way.

One very small mouse
jumped down to the ground
and ran this way and that.

19

He ran so many different ways,
the cat got tired of chasing him
and went back
to whatever he had been doing.

"What a clever little mouse
you are," said Mrs. Brice.
"Now we can go
to buy some food."

Twenty-four little mice

sat in a cart

and enjoyed the ride.

One very small mouse

sat in front.

They went up one aisle.

They went down another.

Mrs. Brice bought

food in cans,

food in jars,

cold food,

hot food.

"Now we can go home,"
said Mrs. Brice.
Twenty-four little mice
were glad.
But one very small mouse
kept on leading the way.
He led them
to the dairy counter.

Mrs. Brice bought
a nice, big cheese.

28

Then she and her mice

went home to eat it.

After they ate
Mrs. Brice sang
and played the piano.

Twenty-four mice
danced around her.

One very small mouse

kept right on eating.